Animals of the Night

SNOW LEOPARDS AFTER DARK

Heather M. Moore Niver

Enslow Publishing
101 W. 23rd Street
Suite 240
New York, NY 10011
USA

enslow.com

Words to Know

chuff—One type of sound that a snow leopard makes.

endangered—In danger of no longer existing.

felines—Animals in the cat family, such as lions, tigers, and leopards.

grazing—Feeding on grasses.

habitat—The place in which an animal lives.

livestock—Animals raised on a farm, such as pigs, horses, or cows.

mammals—Animals that have a backbone and hair, usually give birth to live babies, and produce milk to feed their young.

nocturnal—Mostly active at night.

predators—Animals that kill and eat other animals to stay alive.

prey—An animal hunted by another animal for food.

Contents

Midnight Snack

The snow falls softly high in the mountains of Central Asia. The night darkens. In the shadows something moves. A snow leopard pads through the freshly fallen flakes. Its huge furry paws move it along silently. Suddenly it stops. A sheep is in sight. The large gray-spotted cat creeps closer and closer.

The grazing sheep munches on the grass. The snow leopard pauses and sits perfectly still. When the sheep is close enough, the snow leopard pounces! It grabs the sheep with its front paws. Dinner is served.

FUN FACT!

Snow leopards and house cats are part of the same cat family, called *Felidae*. They are both felines.

Snow leopards can move silently through the snow when they are on the hunt.

Here, Kitty, Kitty

Snow leopards look like great big cats. They weigh between 60 and 120 pounds (27 to 54 kilograms). Snow leopards are 4 to 5 feet (1.2 to 1.5 meters) long. And that doesn't include the tail! A snow leopard's tail adds on another 3 feet (almost 1 m)!

These **mammals** have light gray—almost white—fur with dark circles. Snow leopards have a dark stripe down their backs. They have wide, furry feet that are completely covered with fur. This keeps them warm. Fur on the bottoms of their paws also keeps them from slipping in the snow.

FUN FACT!

Snow leopard feet are just what these animals need to slink through the snow. They work a little like snowshoes.

Snow leopards use their tails
for balance. They also wrap
them around their bodies to
keep warm.

Snow leopards stand 2 feet (0.6 m) tall at the shoulder. Their back legs are long. They are also especially strong. They use this strength to jump along the steep hills in the mountains. A snow leopard can leap up to six times the length of its own body! That's a jump as long as 50 feet (15 m)! Its front legs are shorter. Short legs help them move around the rough mountains more easily.

No one knows how many snow leopards there really are. There might be between 4,500 and 10,000 adults.

Snow leopards lurk all over Asia. They can be found in twelve different countries. They like to hide in the rough, cold mountains. But they are so shy and secretive that most people have never seen one!

A snow leopard's spotted coat of fur is perfect for the snowy **habitat**. The colors help them hide among the rocks and snow. The spots are in rows. They are not as dark in the winter, which helps them blend in with the snow. And it is so nice and thick that it keeps them warm.

FUN FACT!

The snow leopard has a short head and a wide nose. This helps it warm the cold air as it breathes in. This is another handy way to keep warm.

Short ears help the snow leopard keep its body warmer in the cold.

Silent Hunters

Snow leopards are **nocturnal** beasts. Most of their hunting happens at night. They keep pretty busy at dawn and dusk, too. These **predators** are very strong. Snow leopards like to live and hunt in rough, rocky areas. They like steep cliffs, rocks and boulders, and deep valleys. They can jump from boulder to boulder. Here they can stay hidden from their **prey** until it's time to strike. Snow leopards can kill prey that is up to three times their size!

FUN FACT!

In the wild, snow leopards probably only live between ten and thirteen years. In a safe zoo where food is always available, they live up to twenty-two years.

Snow leopards can leap and jump between rocks and keep their footing on steep slopes.

With one leap, snow leopards pounce! Remember, they are super jumpers! They grab their next meal with their front legs. Their long, sharp teeth cut and tear.

Most of their meals include sheep and goats that live in the wild. They will also hunt livestock if prey is hard to come by. Usually snow leopards kill two large animals a month. Hungry snow leopards will also chow down on marmots, birds, and small rodents. They will even eat squirrels.

Snow leopards are well-suited to hunting in the cold, rough mountains. They pounce on their prey with their front legs.

Snow leopards are slow eaters. Sometimes they will take up to three or four days to eat their prey. They always stays nearby to keep other animals from eating the meal they worked so hard for. Vultures and ravens like to try to grab a snack from the dead animal.

Snow leopards don't have a meat-only diet. Have you ever seen your cat eat grass? Snow leopards do, too. They sometimes eat twigs and other leaves as well.

FUN FACT!

Eating grass and plants might help snow leopards digest their food. It might provide vitamins they need, too. Scientists don't know for sure.

Snow leopards balance out their meaty diet by eating grass, twigs, and other plants.

Farmers and Felines

In the winter, food is sometimes hard to find. That's when snow leopards are more likely to hunt livestock. They need to keep themselves fed. But of course farmers aren't happy to have their animals killed. So they hunt snow leopards and defend their farms. Farmers also hunt marmots and other animals that are pests to them. Snow leopards eat these animals to survive, too, so, there is even less for snow leopards to eat. Then they are more likely to hunt livestock. Sometimes snow leopards are hunted for their thick, gorgeous fur, too.

Marmots are pests on the farm, but snow leopards eat them to survive.

Lonesome Leopard

Most snow leopards live on their own. Males and females may get together for a little while to have babies. And a mother will watch over her cubs until they are ready to go out on their own.

Even though they travel alone, snow leopards can cover a lot of land. Their home base might cover hundreds of miles. Because they travel such long distances, snow leopards leave scent markings to tell others where they have been. Sometimes they leave feces or urine. Even rubbing their face against an object can leave a smell for days or weeks.

FUN FACT!

Snow leopards also claw trees and boulders to let other leopards know they were there.

Most of the time, the snow leopard likes his or her own company and

Snow leopards make some noises like a housecat and other big cats. They mew, hiss, growl, moan, and yowl. They even purr. You might expect a big snow leopard to roar like a lion. But they don't! The throat of a snow leopard does not allow them to make a roaring sound. Sometimes snow leopards make a sound with their throat called a "chuff." This is not an aggressive sound. The chuff might even be considered friendly.

Snow leopards can make many noises, but they cannot roar.

Little Kitties

The male snow leopard doesn't hang around to wait for his babies to be born. The female is left on her own. She has to find a safe place to give birth. Usually she finds a place between rocks or a den. She makes it warm and comfortable. The mother covers the den with her fur. She will raise the cubs there, too. Most mothers have two or three cubs. The mother snow leopard gives birth in June or July most often. When the cubs are born they have dark fur.

FUN FACT!

The snow leopard cubs'
eyes are closed for
the first week of
their life.

When they are born, snow leopards need help with almost everything.

When they are first born, snow leopard cubs drink milk from their mother. At two months, the cubs start to eat solid food. They start to run, too. At three months they start to follow their mother. They watch her hunt, and they play at hunting with each other. This is how snow leopard cubs learn to hunt. They live with their mothers for a year and a half. Then it's time to go out on their own.

Snow leopard cubs learn to hunt by pretending to hunt together.

Save the Snow Leopard

Snow leopards are in danger. There are so few left that they are **endangered**. Some are killed by farmers. Others are killed illegally by people who want their gorgeous fur. Still others use parts of their bodies in medicines. Some people make a lot of money with the snow leopard's fur and other parts. Another issue is the land. Humans are taking up more and more space. Their livestock needs more space to graze. This leaves less space for the snow leopard to live.

FUN FACT!

As our planet gets warmer, the cold areas are getting smaller. This leaves fewer places for the snow leopard, too.

Snow leopards need our help and protection if they are going to survive.

Stay Safe Around Snow Leopards

Snow leopards are so shy and hard to spot. You would be lucky to see one. But they are wild animals, not just bigger house cats. Always stay safe around wild animals.

- Farmers have to keep themselves and their animals safe from snow leopards. They build higher fences around where they keep their animals at night.

- Never go out at night if there might be snow leopards around.

- If you have to go out, go in a group of two or more.

- Keep pets and farm animals inside or in a safe place at night.

- Snow leopard cubs are super cute, but they are wild animals, too. And remember their protective mother is probably very nearby, watching and ready to pounce.

- In the very rare instance that you see a snow leopard, don't try to run. It's faster than you! Try and make loud noises and scare it off.

Learn More

Books

Esbaum, Jill. *Explore My World: Snow Leopards*. Washington, DC: National Geographic Society, 2014.

Hatkoff, Craig. *Leo the Snow Leopard*. New York: Scholastic Press, 2010.

Maimone, Sofia. *Snow Leopards in Danger*. New York: Gareth Stevens Publishing, 2014.

Websites

The Alaska Zoo: Snow Leopard

alaskazoo.org/snow-leopard
Learn more with photos and facts about these great cats.

National Geographic: Snow Leopard

animals.nationalgeographic.com/animals/mammals/
snow-leopard/
Read facts and see photos of the shy snow leopard.

The San Diego Zoo: Snow Leopard

animals.sandiegozoo.org/animals/snow-leopard
This site features photos and facts about snow leopards.

Index

Published in 2017 by Enslow Publishing, LLC.
101 W. 23rd Street, Suite 240, New York, NY 10011

Library of Congress Cataloging-in-Publication Data

Names: Niver, Heather Moore, author.

Title: Snow leopards after dark / Heather M. Moore Niver.

Description: New York, NY : Enslow Publishing, 2017 | Series: Animals of the night | Includes bibliographical references and index.

Identifiers: LCCN 2015046918| ISBN 9780766077089 (library bound) | ISBN 9780766077355 (pbk.) | ISBN 9780766076839 (6-pack)

Subjects: LCSH: Snow leopard—Behavior—Juvenile literature. | Snow leopard—Juvenile literature.

Classification: LCC QL737.C23 N58 2016 | DDC 599.75/54—dc23

LC record available at http://lccn.loc.gov/2015046918

Printed in the United States of America

To Our Readers: We have done our best to make sure all website addresses in this book were active and appropriate when we went to press. However, the author and the publisher have no control over and assume no liability for the material available on those websites or on any websites they may link to. Any comments or suggestions can be sent by e-mail to customerservice@enslow.com.

Photo Credits: Throughout book, narvikk/E+/Getty Images (starry background), kimberrywood/Digital Vision Vectors/Getty Images (green moon dingbat); cover, p. 1 andamanec/Shutterstock.com, samxmed/E+/Getty Images (moon); pp. 3, 15 Peter Wey/Shutterstock.com; pp. 5, 21 Dennis W. Donohue/Shutterstock.com; p. 7 Jeannette Katzir Photog/Shutterstock.com; p. 9 Leeloona/Shutterstock.com; p. 11 nialat/Shutterstock.com; p. 13 Paul Dymott/Shutterstock.com; p. 17 JaysonPhotography/iStock/Thinkstock; p. 19 Rudra Narayan Mitra/Shutterstock.com; p. 23 olga_gl/Shutterstock.com; p. 25 DEA/C. DANI I. JESKE/De Agostini/Getty Images; p. 27 © Ardea/Downer, Steve/Animals Animals; p. 29 Abeselom Zerit/Shutterstock.com.